Almost Somebody

poems by

Daniel Roessler

Finishing Line Press
Georgetown, Kentucky

Almost Somebody

Copyright © 2016 by Daniel Roessler
ISBN 978-1-944899-17-2 First Edition
All rights reserved under International and Pan-American Copyright Conventions. No part of this book may be reproduced in any manner whatsoever without written permission from the publisher, except in the case of brief quotations embodied in critical articles and reviews.

ACKNOWLEDGMENTS

Editor: Christen Kincaid

Cover Art: Albert Edwin Roberts, Public Domain

Author Photo: Sam Bond

Cover Design: Elizabeth Maines

Printed in the USA on acid-free paper.
Order online: www.finishinglinepress.com
         also available on amazon.com

Author inquiries and mail orders:
Finishing Line Press
P. O. Box 1626
Georgetown, Kentucky 40324
U. S. A.

Table of Contents

Watermelon Fields ... 1
Pieces of Zero ... 2
Working Class Fathers and Sons ... 3
The City's Darker Side ... 4
The Open Road ... 5
Monsters in Your Mind ... 6
A Man's Worth ... 7
Bus Stop Sally ... 8
My Absent Brother ... 9
Old Friends ... 10
Screaming Into the Night ... 11
Deflowering Daisy Bradstock ... 12
Stutter ... 13
Nobody Lives Forever ... 14
Destination Unknown ... 16
Guilt and Blame ... 17
Where I Grew Up ... 18
My Memory of Roy Finklestein ... 19
Melancholy ... 20
The Lady on the A Train ... 21
Unwanted Guest ... 22
My Empty Garden ... 23
Almost ... 24
Becoming Who I Am ... 25
Steinbeck ... 26
One Day I'll Shine ... 27
I Ask the Maple ... 28

I dedicate this book to all of those struggling to find their place in this world. We are all somebody!

Watermelon Fields

Sinking in the sandy loam
surrounded by black diamonds
no sparkling gems
a different kind of treasure
growing on leafy vines
in Texas summer heat
I bend until my aching back
forces me to stand and stretch
gazing across a thousand rows of green
I sigh and wipe my sweaty brow
on a red handkerchief, nodding my head
toward the day laborer next to me
for we are one in the same
in watermelon fields.

Pieces of Zero

Lofty are the dreams of brown-eyed girls
when they are eighteen and still hold promise,
clutching their prospects like black leather Gucci handbags
but similar to flowers in the garden
potential requires nurturing too
lest it grow into nothing with time,
which can be cruel to the unsuspecting
innocent and unaware of the effort required
to realize imagined possibilities before they trickle away
as easily as rainwater through finger gaps in cupped hands.
Then settling becomes a cold truth
when weariness weighs heavy on pure hearts,
fading smiles and spreading worry lines across tired, anxious faces
until resignation of their loss is acknowledged
and pieces of zero are cherished like diamond engagement rings.

Working Class Fathers and Sons

Before our alarms shrieked a chorus to the day
fathers had already left our neighborhood
wearing steel-toe boots, uniforms, and hardhats
to work in factories, breathing chemicals,
endlessly coughing when they returned home late
sweaty, tired from summer heat and big machines
drinking Miller beer from aluminum cans
reclining in worn leather La-Z-Boys
demanding quiet while watching the late news
and boys like me waited for conversation
hopeful a relationship would come with time
but rent increased requiring more hours,
days grew shorter until I was no longer
around, but off at college living his dream
and the reward for his sacrifice was pride
that he'd made my life better than his own
but as I leave for my office at six a.m.
I know it's not better, just different.

The City's Darker Side

Everybody knows that's Sheila's corner
the one she's worked since she turned fifteen
she stands there in a barely dress and heels
with painted nails and her face on display
like she's attending a masquerade
but she ain't no Cinderella today.
Her arms fold around her to hide the tracks
as she stands and waits, leaning her back
against the graffiti-covered brick wall
with "Jesus" painted in red, white, and blue.
She catches the eye of a passerby
who flashes her a twenty and a smile
so she climbs in his Buick to take her chances
because it's her best offer of the night.
Groping hands awkwardly collide with her flesh
while she closes her eyes and thinks about the time
that one guy took her uptown past the shops
and all those tourists she'd never seen before
since they don't visit her part of the city.

The Open Road

Who knew dishes could be weapons,
sailing through the air in angry fits of rage,
crashing to the floor and shattering
the innocence of a seven-year-old boy,
who scrambles outside seeking refuge
sheltering himself from all the shouting.
He climbs up on his midnight blue Schwinn
and furiously pedals down the street,
hoping to be given wings by the wind
blowing him toward the open road,
where freedom's welcoming arms reach out,
hugging him like loving parents do
when they're not fighting with each other.

Monsters in Your Mind

I never knew,
maybe because I didn't want to,
of how the dark curtains
covered more than the windows
in your room, they veiled your misery,
the chaos in your head,
the loud voices that screamed and
shouted of your worthlessness,
that ripped at your vulnerable soul
tearing it to shreds
and leaving you split down the middle
like an old pair of jeans,
and one became two, neither
of which was you,
and I heard later
about how you wandered the streets
unkempt and unshaven
mumbling and calling out
swatting at the demons all around you
introducing fear as your best friend
and as lonely as I am, I can't imagine
how separated you must have felt
from everyone and everything
that you would run out onto the freeway
in front of speeding cars
to kill the monsters in your mind.

A Man's Worth

I was once an engineer
but would it have made a difference
if I had been a chef or a dogcatcher?
A mechanic or a doctor?
Is my worth in what I do?
Is my worth in a day's pay?
Is my value that I carry grocery bags
into the house after shopping, or
that I take the trash out at 6 a.m.
before the garbage men come by
in their huge, loud truck
to haul away the remnants of our lives,
all the while shaking their heads
at the meager contents.
I've tried to change,
morph into another man
more to your liking
but his reflection in my mirror
is vacant.
I have learned in the process
my worth is anchored to myself—
tethered to my own afflictions.

Bus Stop Sally

Her silver hair shimmers in the blistering sun
and she might be getting a burn
but who could tell with all that blush.
She wears a flowery dress every day
even when it's raining.
And she totes around that black leather purse,
which long ago went out of style,
clings to it tight like it's one of her children
that she hasn't seen in thirty years
because she walked out on them
and the white picket fence life she had.
She scurries to the bus when it arrives
like she's in a hurry and has someplace to go
but riding the bus around town all day
is a journey, not a destination.

My Absent Brother

You have stalked me since birth
like my trailing shadow in the sun.
Your name falls from Father's tongue
far too often to be a distant memory.
You are present in Mother's melancholy,
an unspoken sorrow lingering in the room.
And many, many winters have passed
but they still remember.

You are the source of my greatest doubt—
that another boy would not be necessary—
but in your passing my life originated.
Burdening me with unwanted responsibility,
you taunt me with your idyllic image
pointing out my own imperfections.
And so many times, I have questioned
without any answers.

You whisper to me in my slumber
with brotherly guidance and advice
for which I have often yearned.
You are much more like our father,
interested in cattle and cars
but still we are more the same, than not.
And because of that I miss you
my absent brother.

Old Friends

Night creeps in
through slits in the blinds
I am swallowed up
by my King size bed
naked, alone
self-conscious, inadequate.
A blanket of darkness
begins to smother me
so I reach backwards
and pluck a memory
to keep me company.
Do you remember walking
in the rain? Sharing dreams
and anticipating tomorrows
to deliver on the promises
we'd made. But ten years later,
I saw you on the street
and you acted like you didn't recall
my name or that we went to school together.
And since, I've often wondered,
if I were rain and poured myself out
would I have been somebody
who meant something
to you?

Screaming into the Night

That reckless, crazy crackhead three doors down
stands in her front yard at two a.m.
screaming that the night swallowed her children
and from my window I see her pot-smoking boyfriend
on their front porch, once again getting high,
convinced he's doing nothing wrong
since the President said it's okay.
And her children…they are safe for now,
finally being fed and taken care of.
CPS came three nights ago and took them,
and I hope they don't return
because she always thinks it's someone else's fault
that she don't have a job, that she's an addict,
that her life is crappy. And I'm sick of all
her misplaced blame.
I scream into the night "Shut Up!"
but nobody listens.

Deflowering Daisy Bradstock

It's easy to invent the truth and sell it
to teenage girls who long to be beautiful,
falsely believing first loves last forever
and happy endings happen in real life.
Daisy's eyes were just plain brown, nothing special,
peering out from behind oversized glasses,
perched on a nose that was far too flat
and covered with a field of reddish freckles.
Sandy hair in layers and in waves,
a few extra pounds in the middle,
and emerging breasts, ripe for the plucking.
A date night when we skipped the movie
to park at the overlook in my old Chevy.
I whispered out the words "I love you"
which mesmerized her like the sparkling stars
and I meant it in that briefest of moments.
She let her walls crumble and we embraced,
caressed by the hand of our freedom in the night
as the radio played a rhythmic love song,
one she thought was written just for her.
And when our love was done, she pulled on her skirt,
checked her makeup and smiled a toothy smile,
failing to recognize what she had lost in my arms.
Daisies only bloom once, before withering and wilting.

Stutter

Twisted and mangled words
catch and hold my tongue
for a moment too long,
before they fall away
tumbling through the air
like acrobats in Cirque de Soleil
and you stare,
confused, or maybe amused,
and my self-consciousness grows
into scarlet embarrassment
until I'm strangled by it
choking on the gurgling sound
of my dying desire
to ever speak again.

Nobody Lives Forever

Yesterday, Miss Mattie said she don't know—
Why these young men wear pants down
around their knees and show their butt cracks
to everybody like it's supposed to be that way. Why
these teenage girls dress like prostitutes and put
their business out there for all to see.
Why hard work seems to be a crime these days
and welfare's considered a job. She picked cotton
when she was a little girl, and then cleaned houses
when she grew up. Wasn't glamorous, but she did okay,
raised four kids and sent 'em to college. All of 'em
except Alfred are doing alright. He got mixed up with
a floozie out of Atlanta, she screwed him in bed,
then got him to drinking, then screwed him in the divorce.
Came to Thanksgiving one year dressed up like a ten dollar whore.
Called herself a vegetarian, refused to eat the turkey.
Who don't eat turkey on Thanksgiving?
Alfred never was her smartest. And hell,
she's damn near eighty-three now, owns her own place.
Isn't much, just a shack on the edge of Jackson,
but it's home. Has been since 1971.
Can't figure out why people need these big houses.
Half of 'em got bathrooms bigger than her kitchen.
Why the hell anybody need a bathroom that big?
Don't take that much space to take a shit. And
she's been wondering why church pews are getting empty.
Reverend Jenkins says the end times are near. He might be right,
seems like these people today need God more than ever,
but don't know it.
Mr. Tom sold his ice cream shop last month.
It's just around the corner from the post office,
and she treats herself to a double scoop of butter pecan
once a month.

New owner's a foreigner, wears a sheet around his head.
Stared at her when she went in last week and she didn't much like it.
Yep, that's what Miss Mattie told me.
I found her dead in bed this morning, wearing a pink silk
nightgown that was perfect against her ebony skin.
Cat was crawled up near her feet. She loved that damn cat.

Destination Unknown

This vagabond dreams of catching wind
gliding across endless blue to blend
into the horizon far away
which melts into the approaching day.

This hopeful seeker searches for new
awaiting comets in midnight blue
bright flashes that quickly diminish
leaving no remnants once they finish.

This carefree wanderer makes his way
moving swiftly, never long to stay
like vivid autumn leaves on display
decaying into the cold winter gray.

This sailor drifts both river and sea
finding out how rough waters can be
in white rapids and waves tossed about
drenched in uncertainty, filled with doubt.

This lonely traveling man I know
I've often watched him come and go
and still he journeys on alone
toward a destination unknown.

Guilt and Blame

I stand at the one-lane bridge
floating above Five Mile Creek
in the jumping off place
where I watched you become a memory
melting into the wind
and fluttering away like a butterfly.
And there isn't enough blame to go around.

Where I Grew Up

There were no high-rise apartments
where I grew up
in a small town
with a few traffic lights and
a couple of Mexican restaurants
too many convenience stores
and fast-food joints.
Summers were hot and
winters were sparse
where I grew up
in South Texas.
Pump jacks from another time
resembled big metal grasshoppers
bowing their heads as I drove by
in my powder blue pickup truck.
Friday nights were for football games
where I grew up
in the stadium's shadow
the players were gods
worshipped
for their inherited athletic prowess
while those of us who didn't play
were nothing
but ignored.

My Memory of Roy Finklestein

Roy Finklestein took our dare
to prove to us he belonged
but carefree summers of youth
can be darkened by hauntings,
from subtle movements in windows
of vacant green houses
on barren corner lots
tempting boys to become men,
confronting their fears by
opening doors and walking through.
When Roy caught a glimpse
of creeping shadows in the blackness,
imaginary monsters chased away his courage
and after he wet his pants
he sprinted home crying
making it clear a boy was still a boy.
And we all laughed, relieved it wasn't us.

Melancholy

I once caught a brief glimpse of happiness
as it ran away from me like the basset hound pup
I got when I was ten, and I didn't understand, then
or now, so I sat on my front porch from May to August
awaiting a return that never came. Melancholy,
a weighty emotion that is so misunderstood,
became my constant companion and we sat together
at tables in restaurants sharing dinner. People stared
at our odd marriage that left an unmistakable void
in the straight back chair across from me
but they never let their whispers become questions
because they didn't want the answers,
which might have caused them moments of discomfort.
And only a week ago, as we drove home listening to the radio,
mostly sad songs of lover's laments and the blues,
there on the side of the road was where we parted ways,
when I found a wandering puppy and took it for my own.

The Lady on the A Train

She stands near but seems afar
blending in with the blur
of scattered, distant, partial memories,
reminding me of someone I once knew.
I wonder if her willingness to be forgotten
is a desperate attempt to be remembered.
Her eyes blink out a somber melody,
which she betrays with the swaying of her head,
but to the stranger watching, it is out of rhythm—
an awkward symphony of nothingness.
She swims her hand into a fake Louis Vuitton
and plucks crimson lipstick from the disarray,
applying it to pursed lips that don't require
the decadence of a substitute facade.
In younger years, she might have been somebody
worth knowing, but that time has faded like her jeans,
and as she steps off the train at the last stop,
she doesn't even bother waving goodbye.

Unwanted Guest

I didn't ask you to come
but you showed up anyway
and now you taunt me
like my sister did when I was a boy
but her mocks were in jest
not malicious and hateful like yours.
Your grip upon my throat is tight
and I wriggle with myself
trying to break free
but self-loathing's grasp is unyielding,
so I sharpen the edges of the blade
of my being and cut against the grain
of sand and water of which I'm made
until I fall through the narrow pass
of the hourglass to disappear like time,
voiding my existence.

My Empty Garden
A Gogyohka

I planted seeds
they blossomed
showing great promise
caterpillars invaded
now I begin again.

Almost

I stand on the edge
of promise,
on the brink
of breaking through,
alone
with my potential
eager to shine,
stretching my arms out
anxious to grasp the brass ring,
the cusp is here beside me,
my destiny awaits
but I never quite get over
the emptiness that comes
from always being
next in line.

Becoming Who I Am

In your shadow I am lost
a dark stain on a dark stain
indistinguishable
where is my identity?
WHO AM I?
I press my face against
your outline
and even if it only gives
a little is a lot.
I push the boundary—
reshape myself
and like a balloon pricked
by a straight pin
you deflate as I take shape
growing into the courage
to be me
and shedding the cloak
of my former self.

Steinbeck

When you rose in Salinas I didn't know you
I wasn't born yet and wouldn't be for many years
so how did we become friends?
It was because you were fearless in letting me in,
giving me a piece of you on every single page.
Character! With you it was all about character
and how each of us is a part of someone else
and they in turn are a part of us
long before we are astute enough to know it.
Family, my father was born in 1939,
the year of *The Grapes of Wrath*
and when I was an awkward teenage boy
eager to experience the world,
the Joads visited and changed me,
giving birth to a dream that my words
would one day contain the power of yours.
And maybe it will never be so, or maybe
tomorrow I will dive deep and find Kino's pearl,
either way you have given me that hope
and I am all the better for it.

One Day I'll Shine
—Golden Shovel of Daffodils by William Wordsworth

The truth about me is that I
have often wondered and wandered,
trying to escape my lonely,
which clings to me just as
tightly in a crowded room as in a
barren field under cover of a dark cloud,
hovering and continuous.
And I wait for my moment as
if its someone else's responsibility, the
happiness that eludes me like the stars
but it is in my waiting that
I'm polished, and can finally begin to shine.

I Ask the Maple

Autumn passes slowly
for a man resistant to change
hiking on the limestone ridge near dusk
when a wicked breeze finds its fury
and pokes through the pores
of my pale, uncovered face.
A blanket of mist adds to my misery
causing me to wonder if what I came here looking for
is already gone for good. My back aches
and my knees throb like those of most old men
but it's my empty soul that hurts the most,
weary of struggling against myself.
I settle against the furrowed trunk
look up in admiration at the color collage
of my umbrella. The spidery veins of the leaves
flowering out on yellow, brown and red canvases.
And I ask the Maple,
"How do you have such splendor and magnificence,
when I have nothing?"
An answer rustles from the branches above,
"This is my season, soon it will be yours."
I stand and walk away, content
to wait for winter.

Daniel **Roessler** is an author and poet who grew up in a small town in rural South Texas. Inspired by the poetry of Robert Frost, Daniel began writing poems in his early teens. He has continued studying the craft of poetry and is an active participant in *Writer's Digest Poetic Asides* challenges where his poems have placed in numerous competitions.

Daniel is a member of The Writer's League of Texas and the Academy of American Poets. In July 2014, he contributed a three-part guest blog series for *Writer's Digest Poetic Asides* on nature poems. In addition to poetry, he is an aspiring mystery/thriller author.

Previous publishing credits include one nonfiction book and numerous magazine articles on a variety of topics. Daniel currently resides in Austin, Texas.

www.ingramcontent.com/pod-product-compliance
Lightning Source LLC
Chambersburg PA
CBHW060226050426
42446CB00013B/3182